Beloved
Words

Coloring Book

Illustrated by Heidi McKee

Written by God Almighty

DEDICATION

I honestly can't believe this is happening! God has truly given me joy in His salvation and
I am super excited to share this book with others! May you experience the Peace of God
that transcends all comprehension as you color and meditate on His Beloved Word!

My sister, Tammy Grinn, has inspired me all of my life! From her self-sacrificing love to her down right hard
work ethic, she always LOVES passionately! She encouraged me to pursue this little project and spent many
hours researching and editing. I hope to give grand proceeds from the sale of this book to help her and her
husband's adoption fund as they pursue another set of parentless children to love!

My Mom is the most creative person I know!
I am thankful to God that she taught me to love creativity and God's Word.

Lastly, I dedicate this to the many parentless kids hoping to find their forever homes.

"Religion that God our Father accepts as pure and faultless is this: to look after
orphans and widows in their distress and to keep oneself from being polluted by the world."
James 1:27

These Pages have not been digitally enhanced.
The artwork is completely free-hand and one of a kind originals.
Try one yourself!

"Jesus looked at them and said, "With man this is impossible, but with God all things are possible." Matthew 19:26

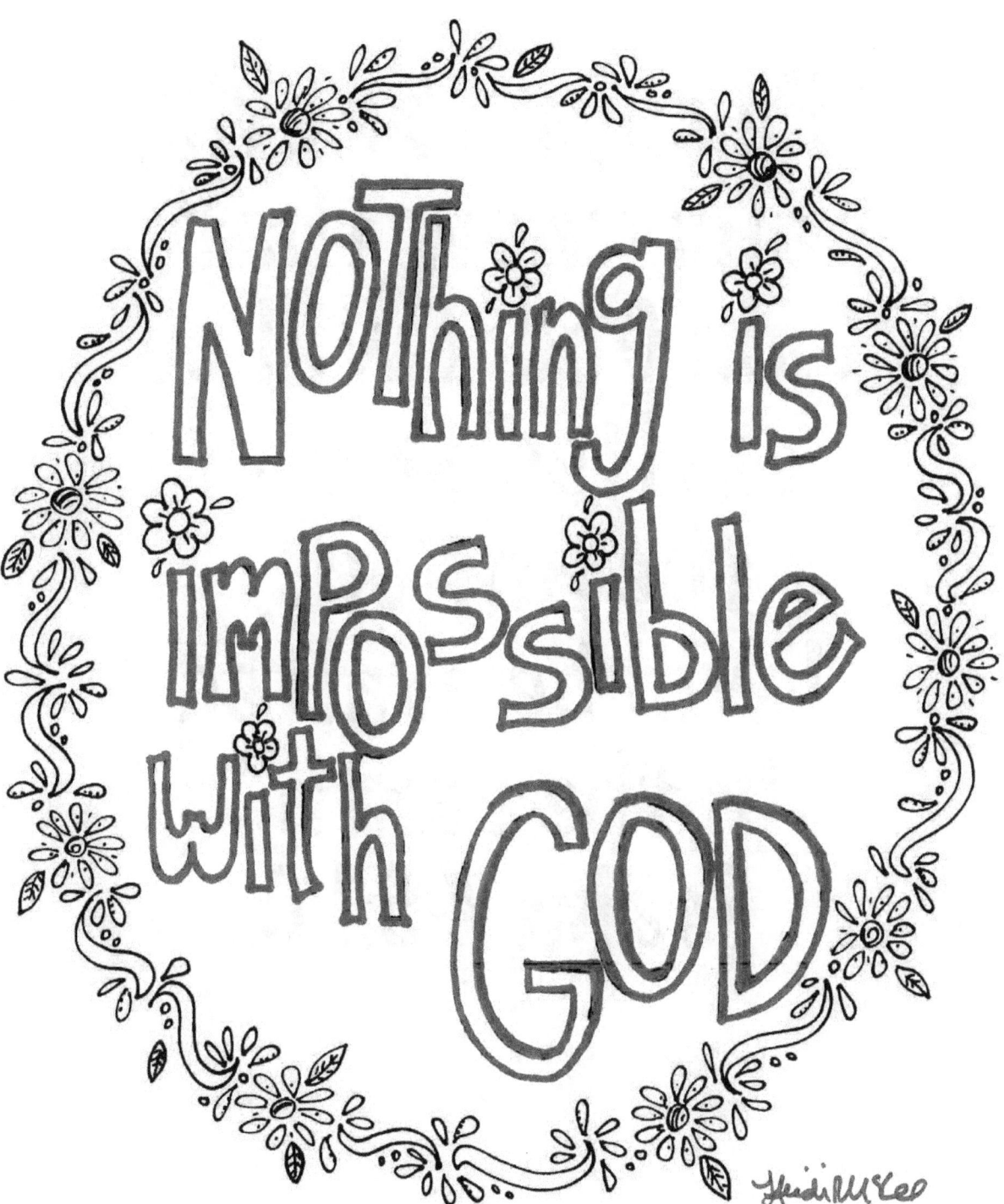

"He says, "Be still, and know that I am God; I will be exalted among the nations, I will be exalted in the earth."
Psalm 46:10

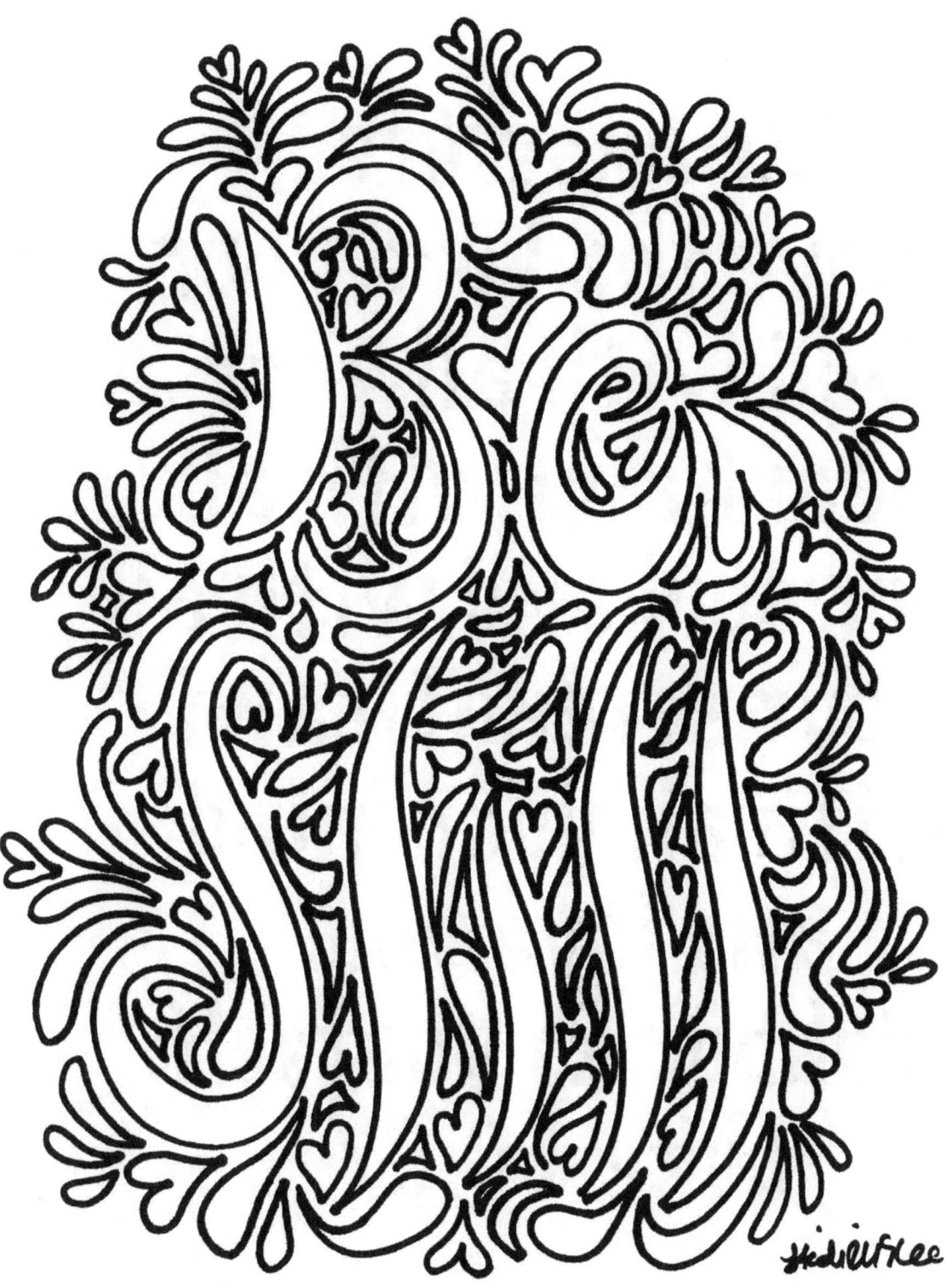

"He answered,
"Love the Lord your
God with all your
heart and with all
your soul and with all
your strength and
with all your mind;
and love your
neighbor as yourself."
Luke 10:27

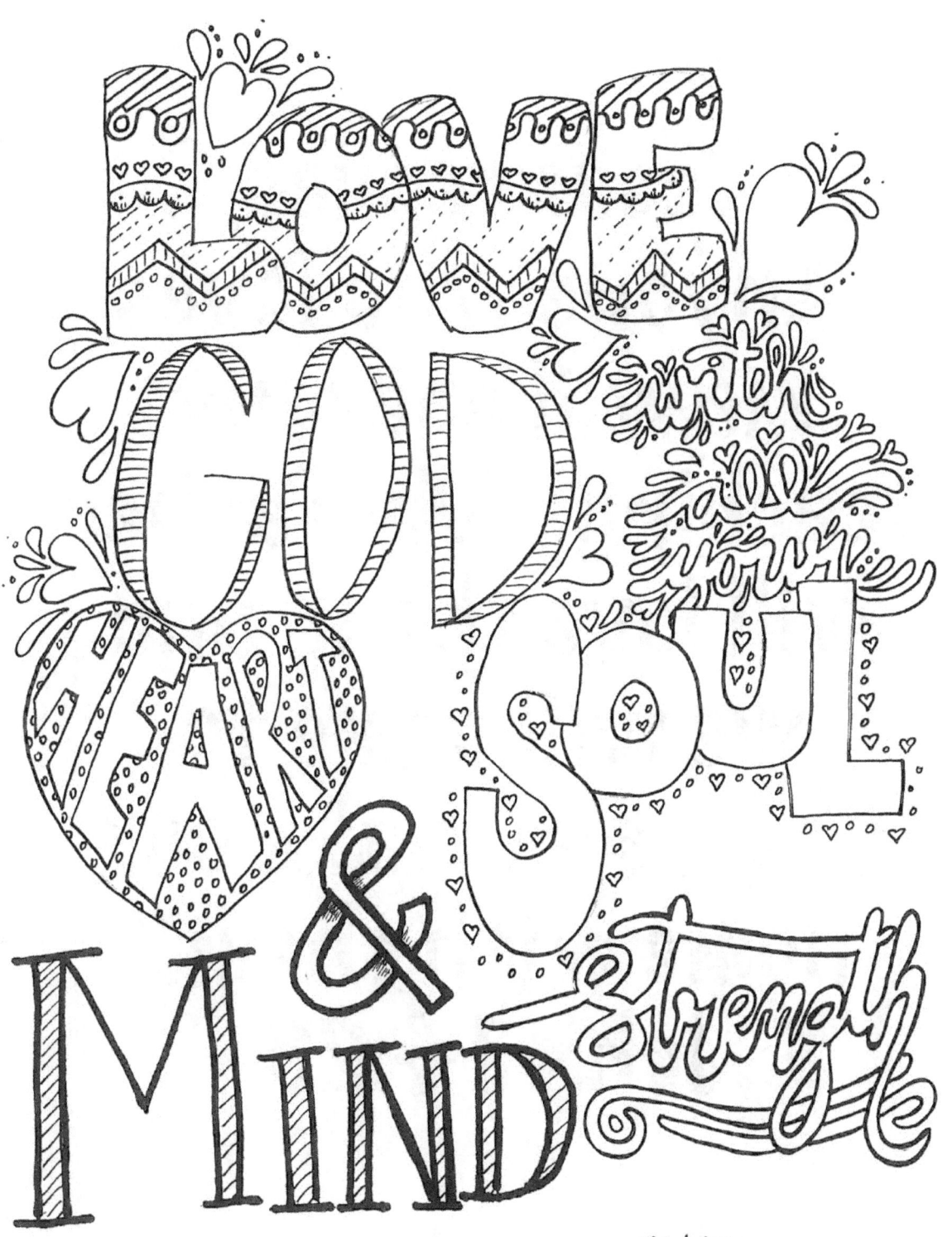

"Jesus replied, "Anyone who loves me will obey my teaching. My Father will love them, and we will come to them and make our home with them."
John 14:23

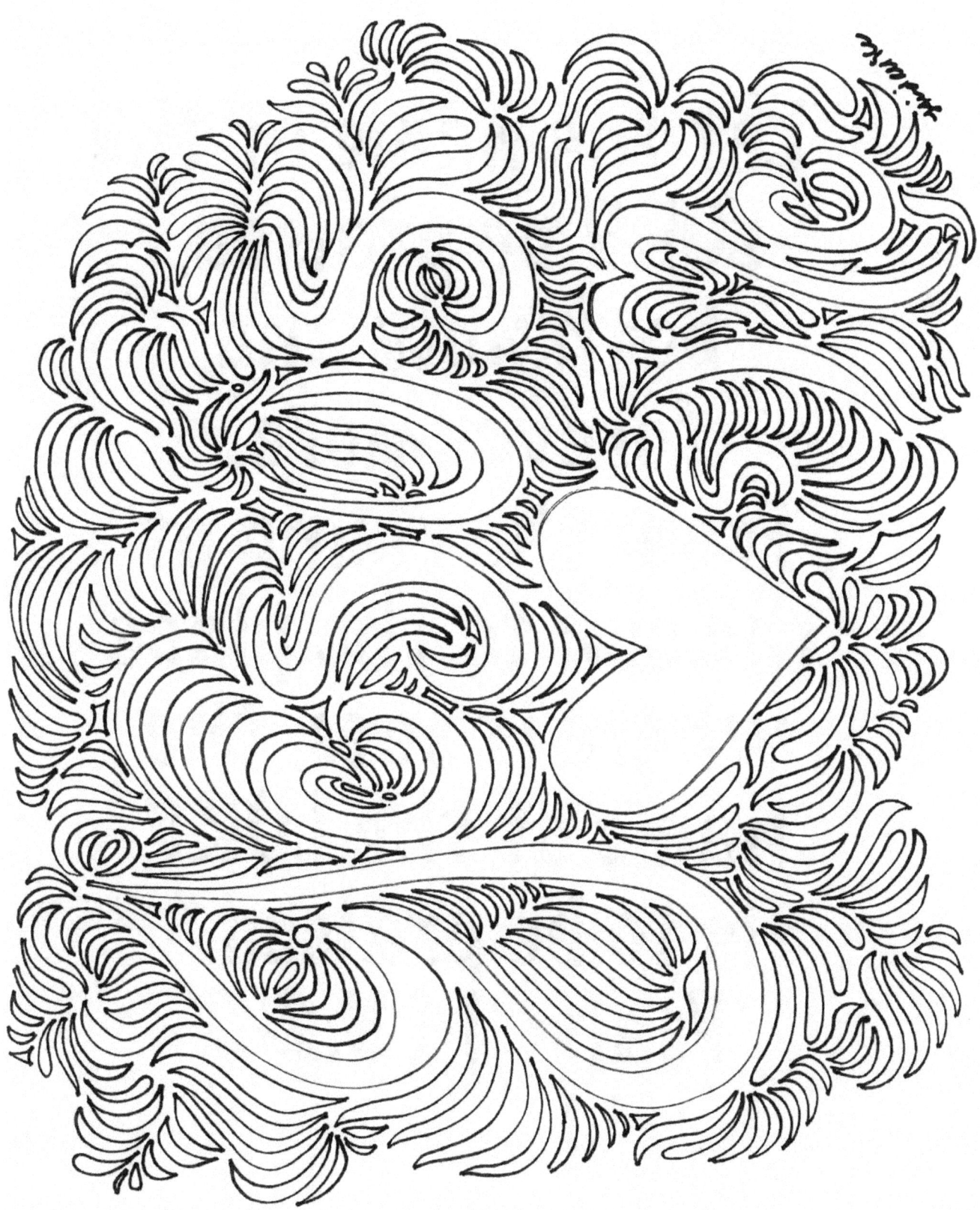

"Let the name of the LORD be praised, both now and forevermore. From the rising of the sun to the place where it sets, the name of the LORD is to be praised."
Psalm 113:2-3

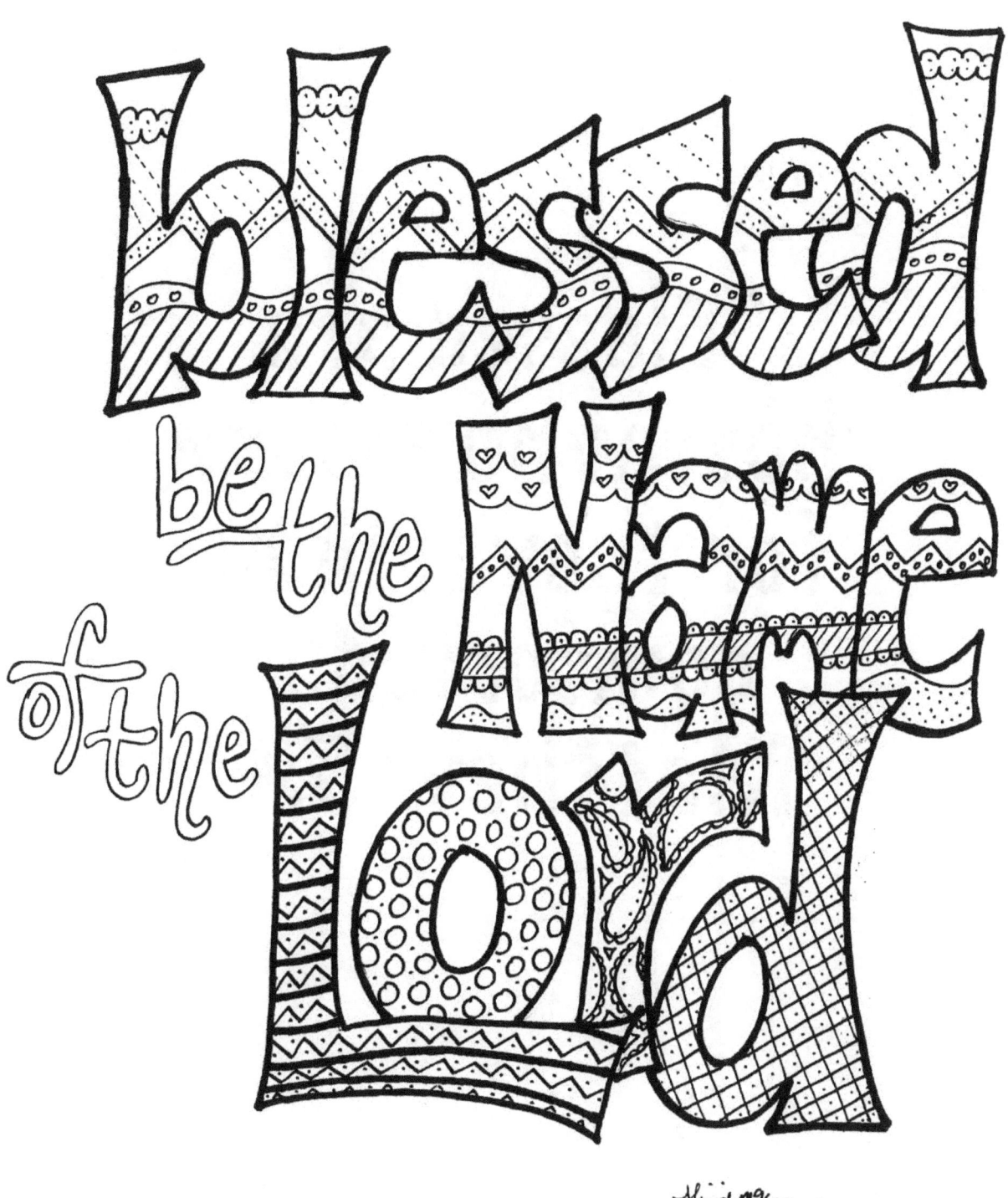

"Blessed are those who mourn, for they will be comforted."
Matthew 5:4

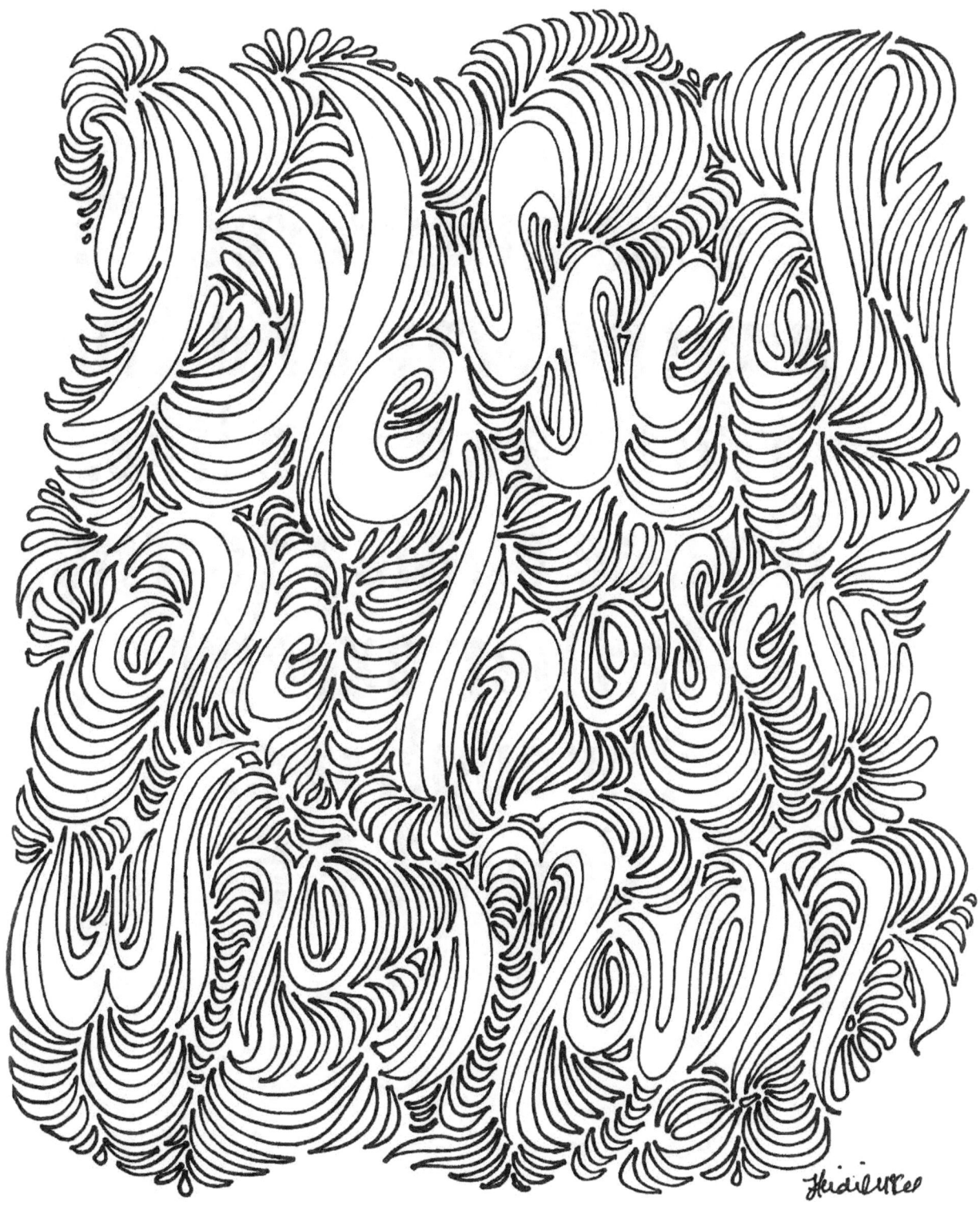

"Jesus answered, "I am the way and the truth and the life. No one comes to the Father except through me."
John 14:6

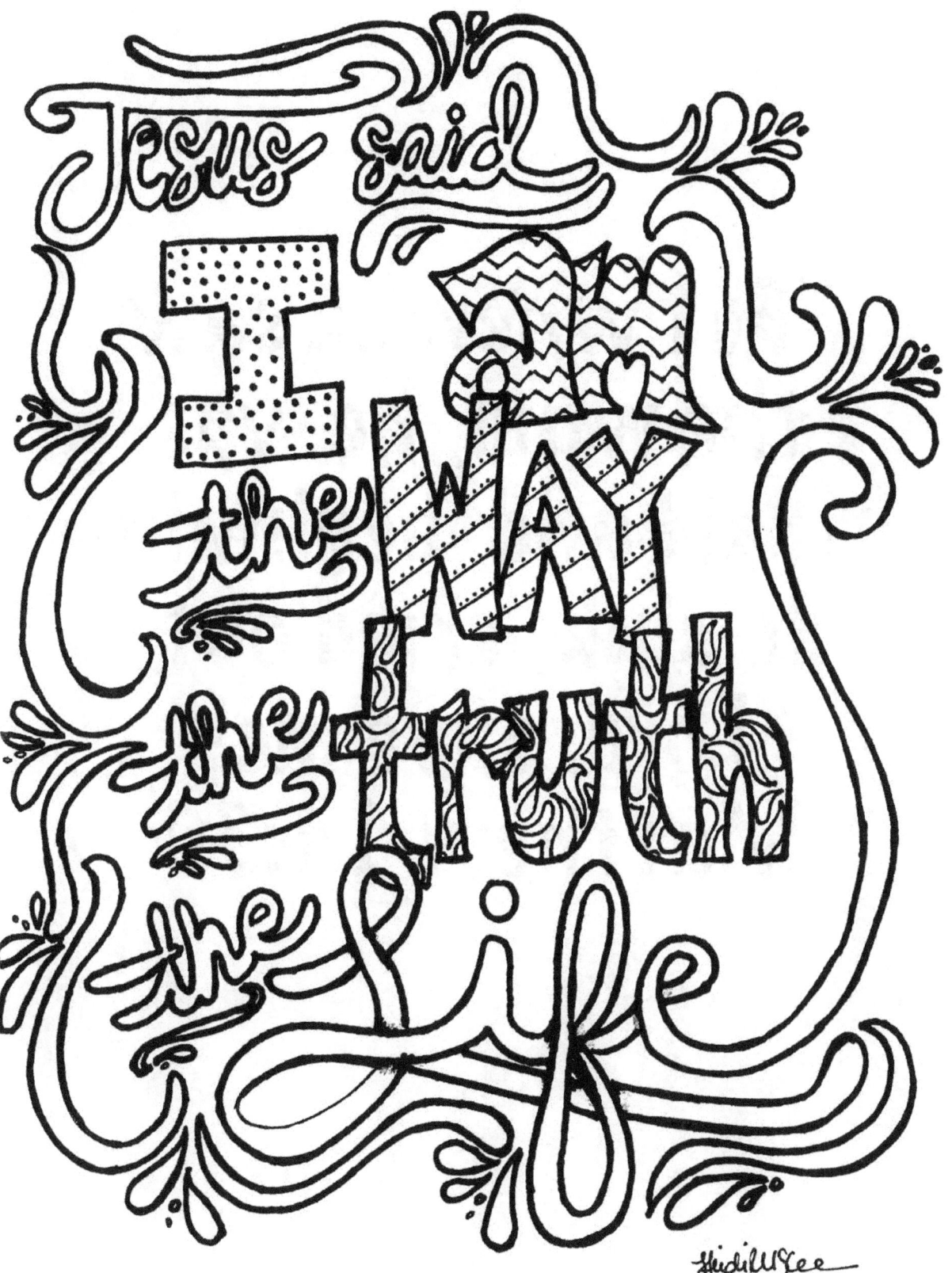

"But when he saw the wind, he was afraid and, beginning to sink, cried out, "Lord, save me!" Matthew 14:30

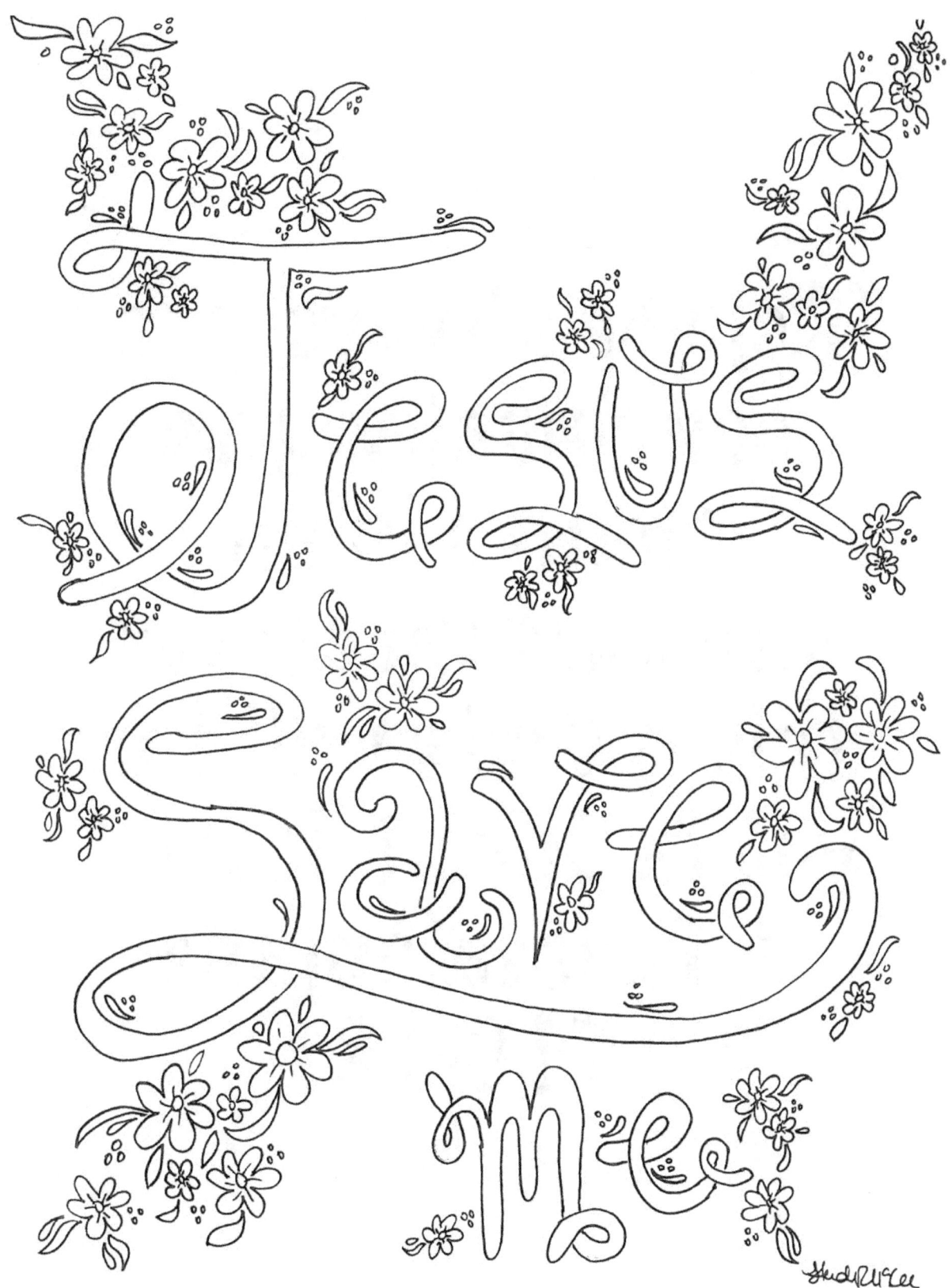

"Rejoice always, pray continually, give thanks in all circumstances; for this is God's will for you in Christ Jesus." 1 Thessalonians 5:16-18

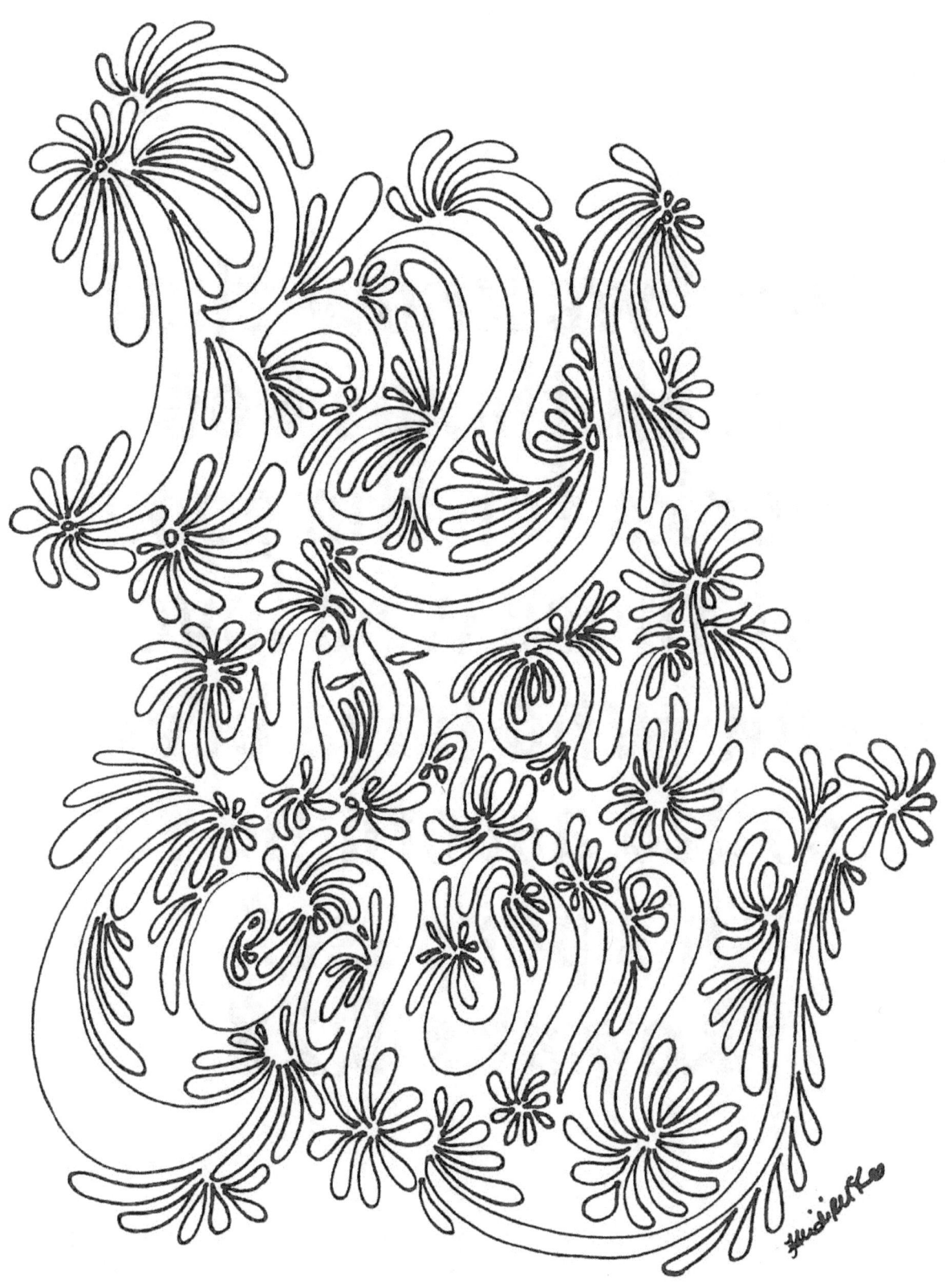

"And we know that in all things God works for the good of those who love him, who have been called according to his purpose." Romans 8:28

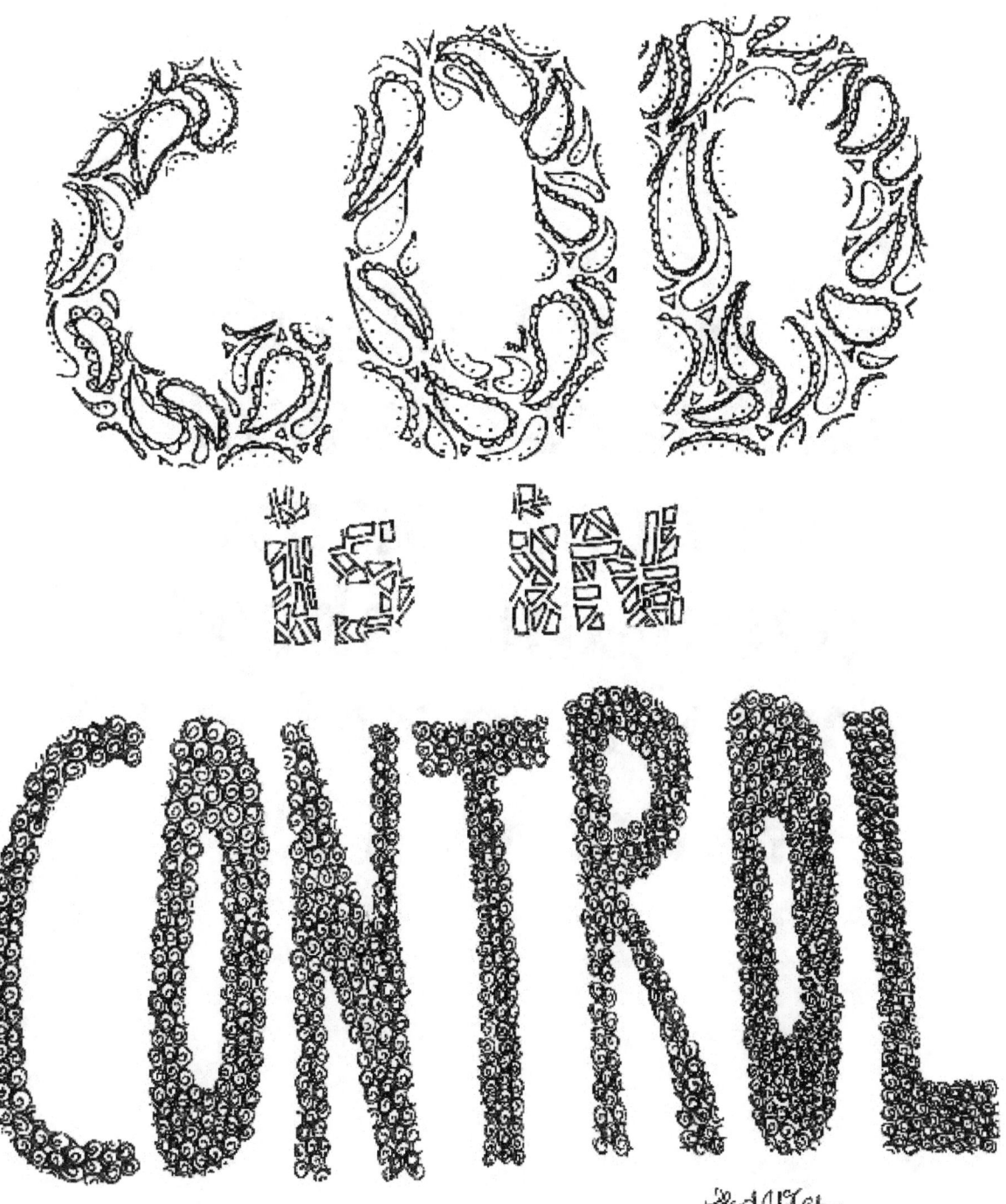

"Now faith is confidence in what we hope for and assurance about what we do not see." Hebrews 11:1

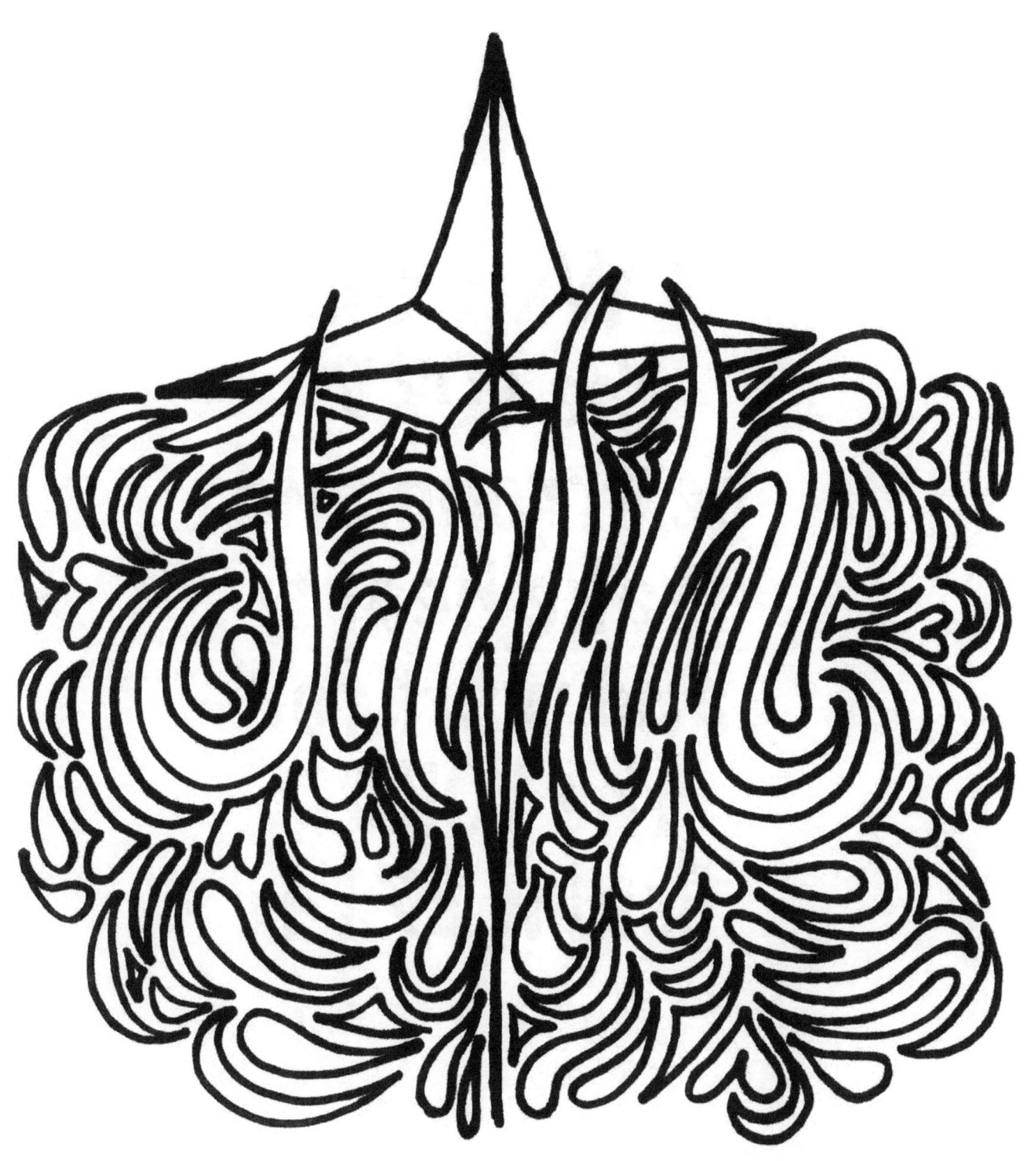

"Wait for
the LORD;
be strong and
take heart
and wait for
the LORD."
Psalm 27:14

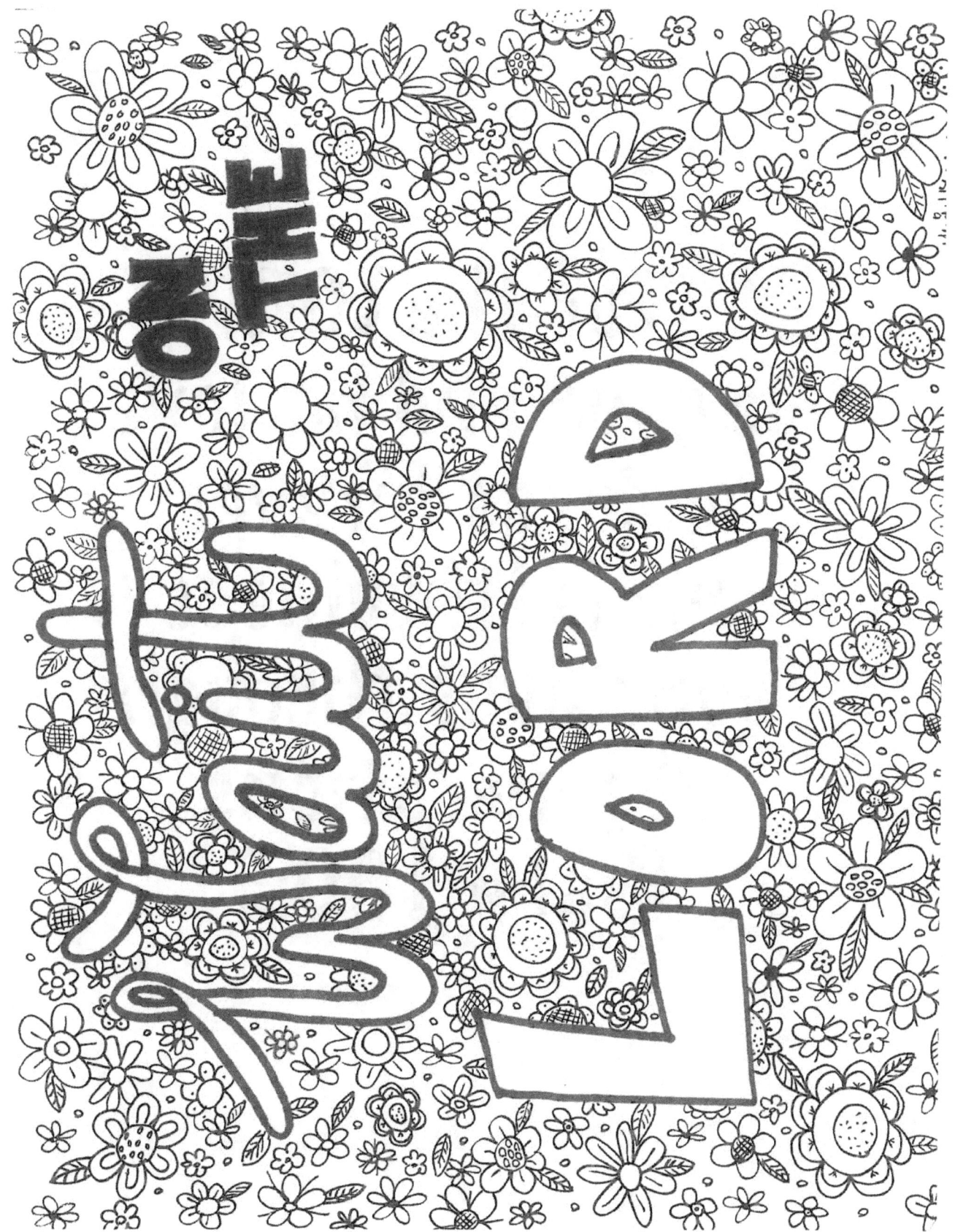

"For the LORD
is good and his love
endures forever;
his faithfulness
continues through
all generations."
Psalm 100:5

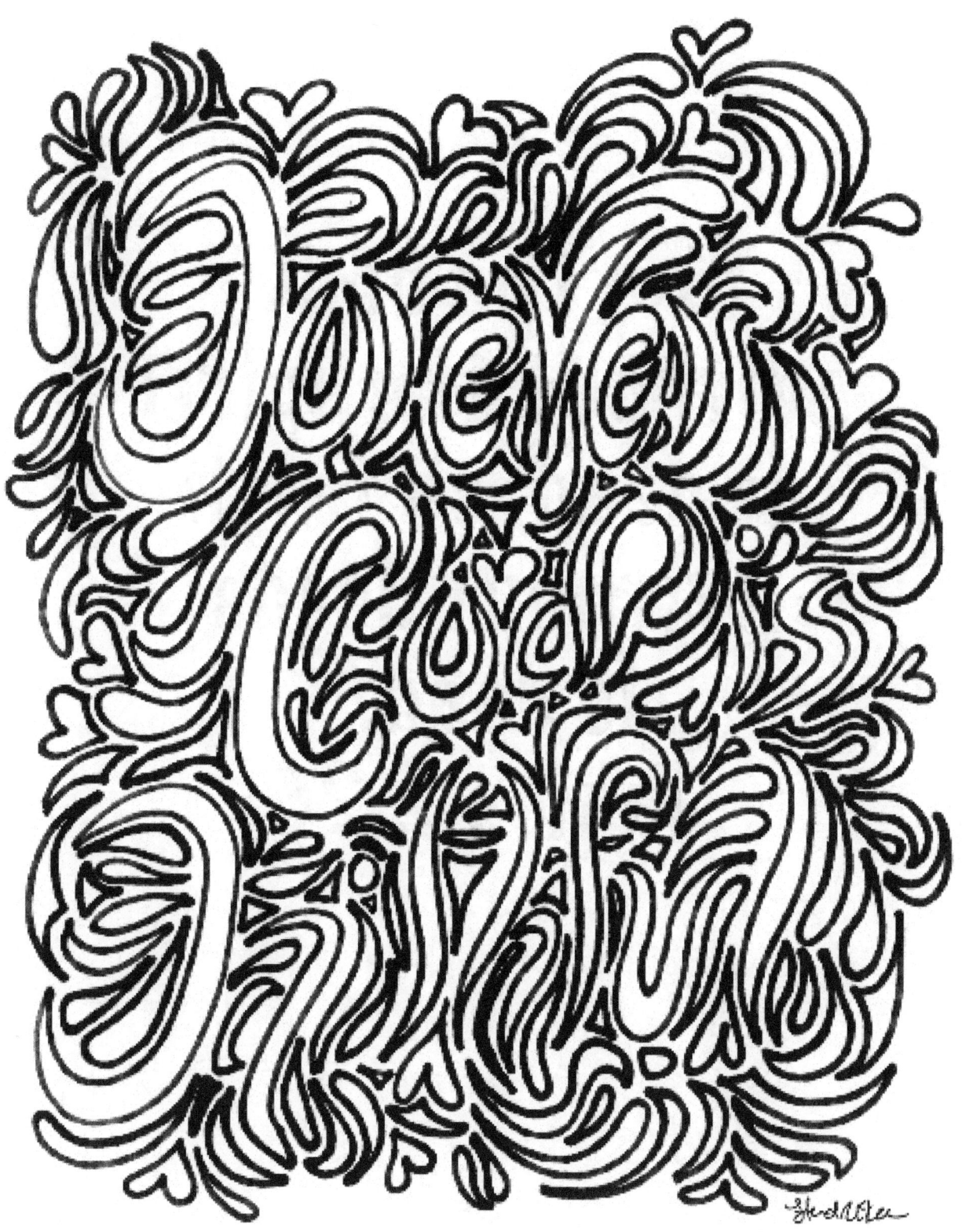

"As the body
without the spirit
is dead, so faith
without deeds
is dead."
James 2:26

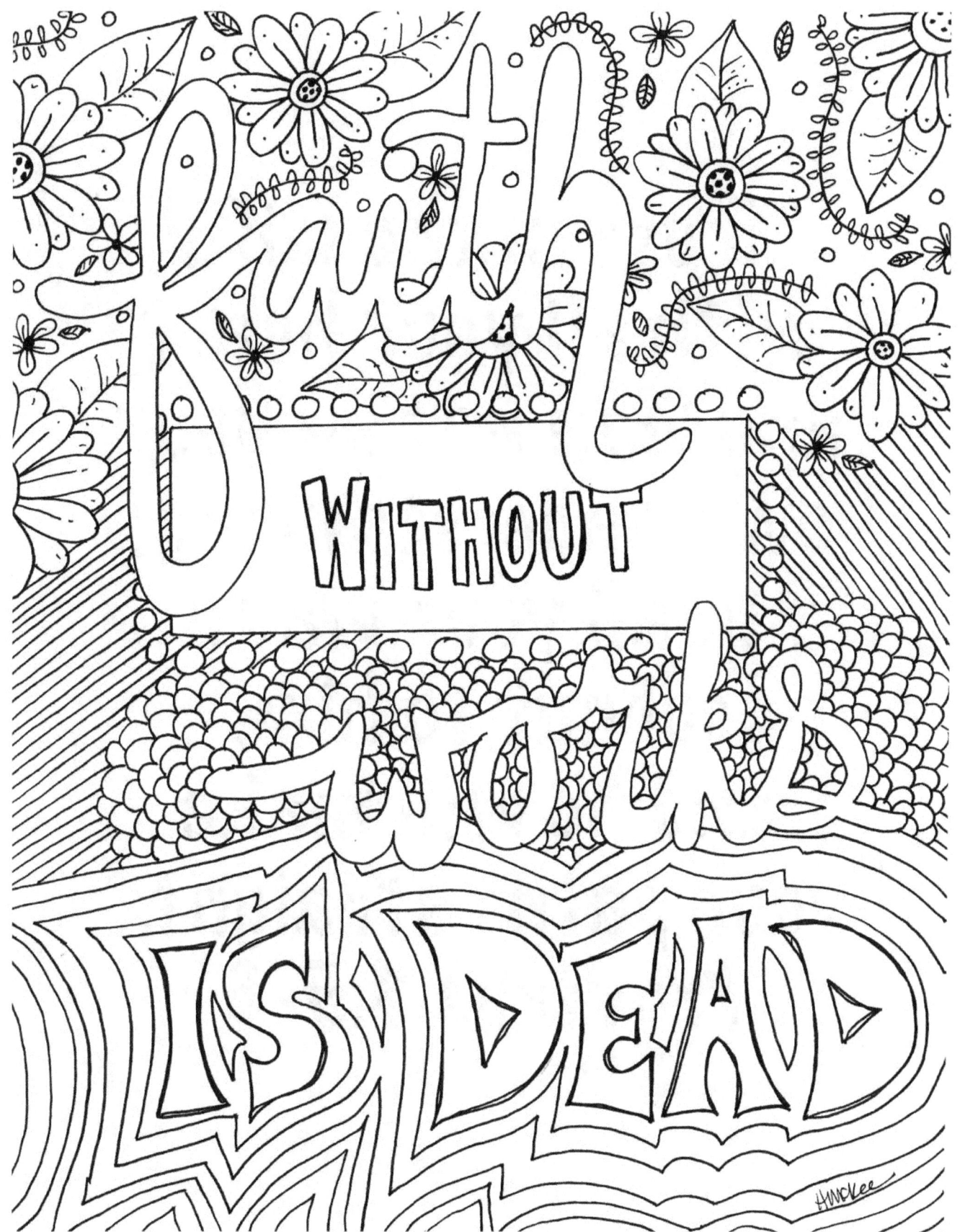

"Trust in the LORD with all your heart and lean not on your own understanding; in all your ways submit to him, and he will make your paths straight." Proverbs 3:5-6

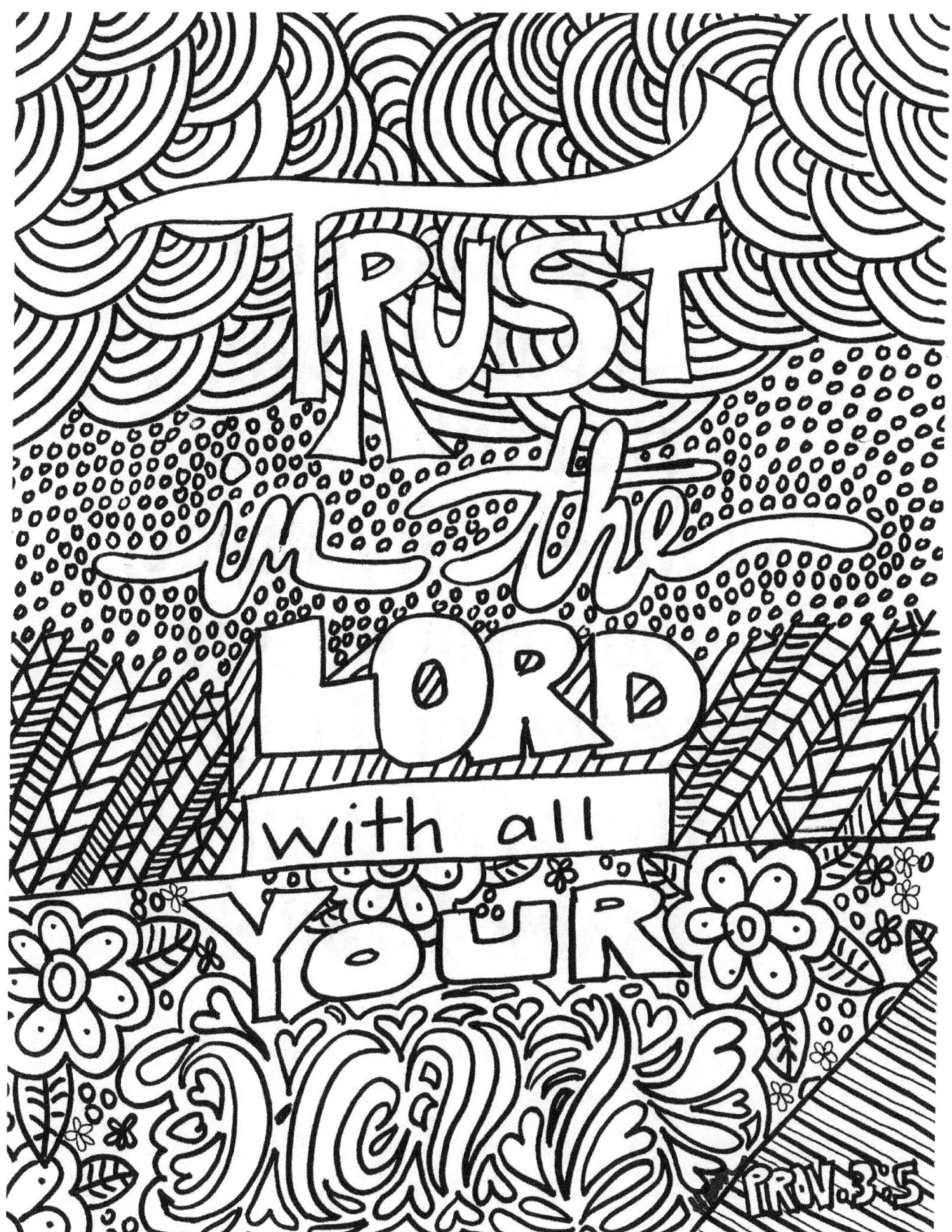

"I praise you because I am fearfully and wonderfully made; your works are wonderful, I know that full well."
Psalm 139:14

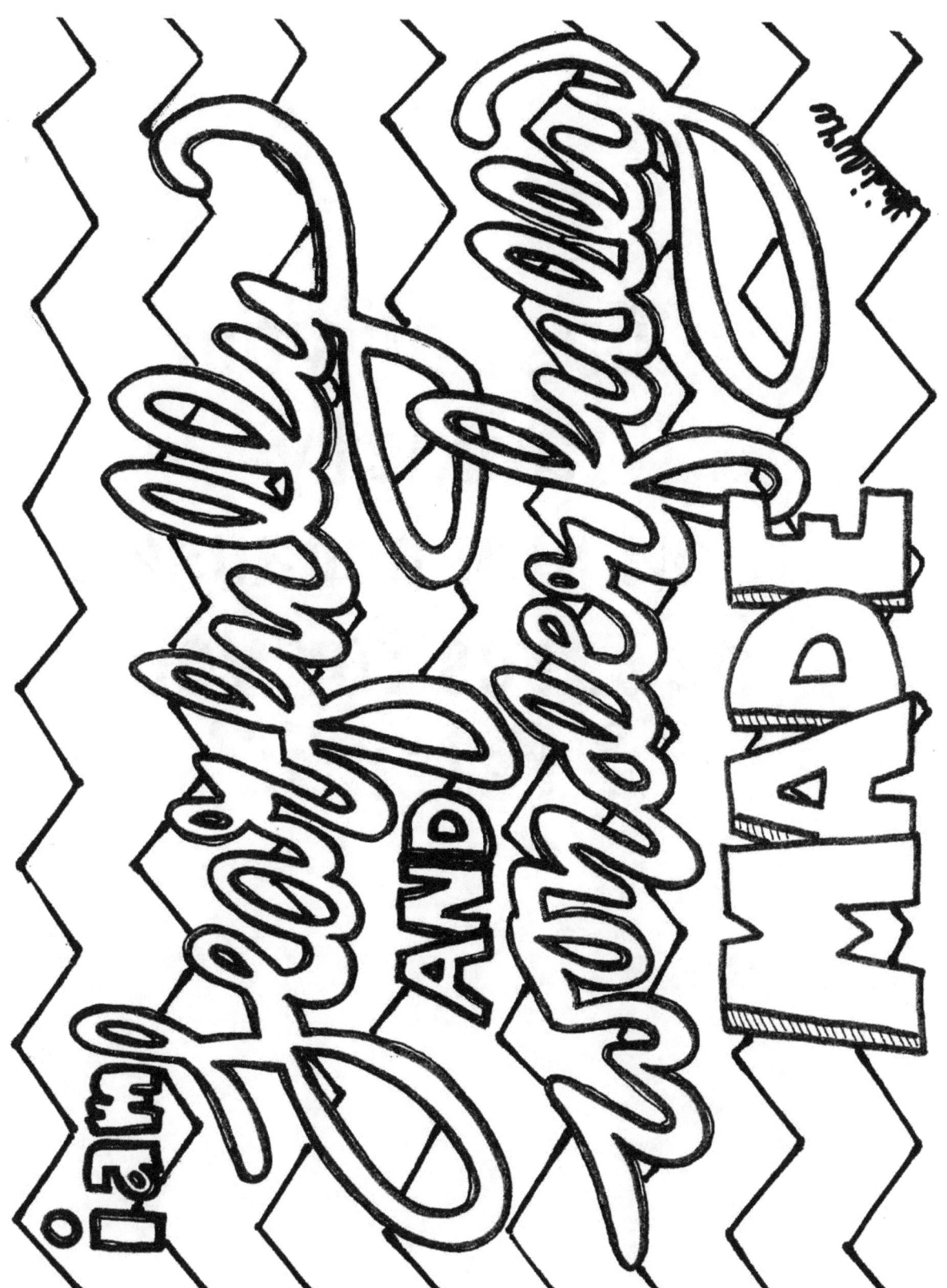

"Cast all your
anxiety
on him because
he cares for you."
1 Peter 5:7

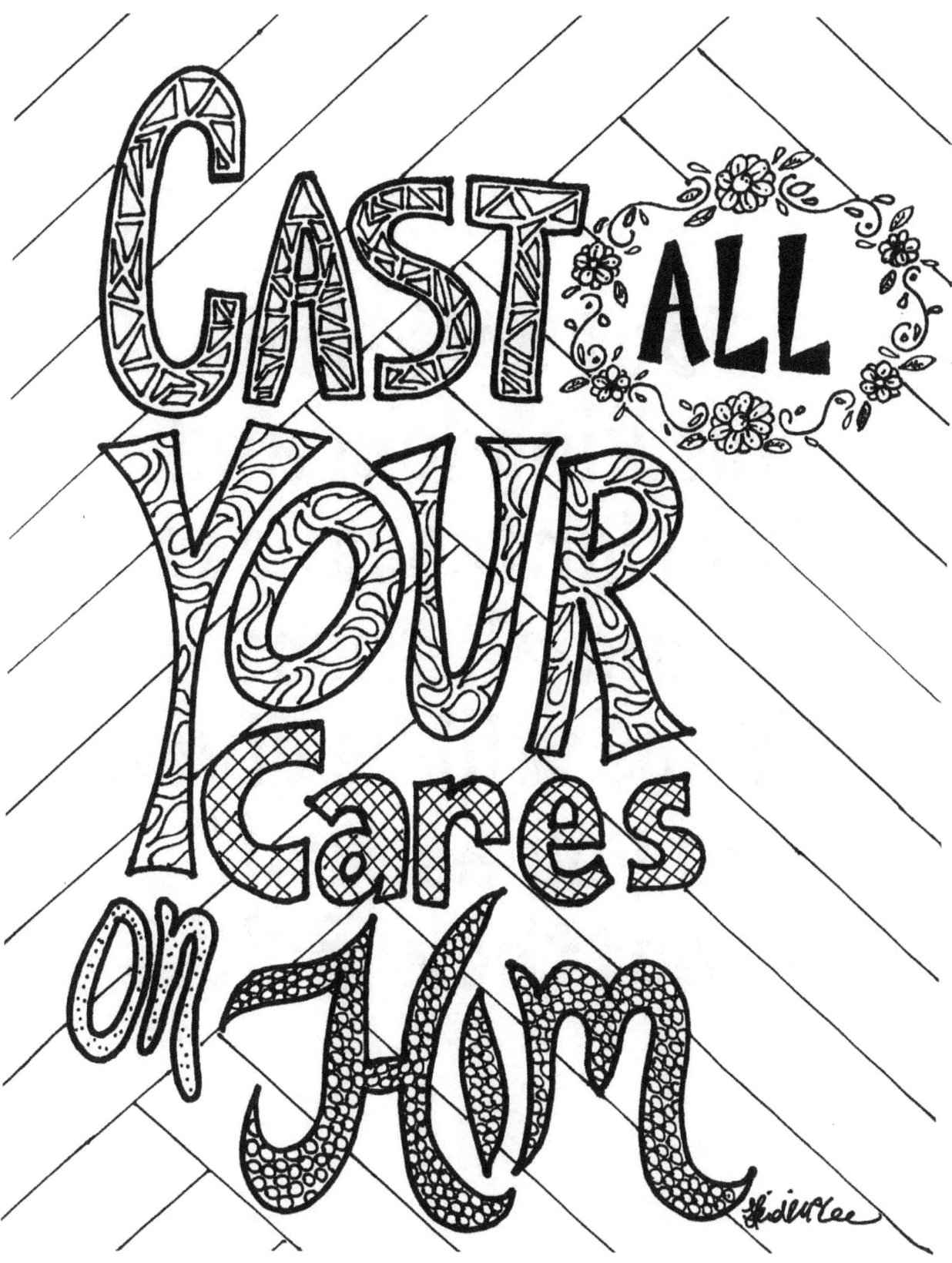

"But seek first
his kingdom and
his righteousness,
and all these
things will be given
to you as well."
Matthew 6:33

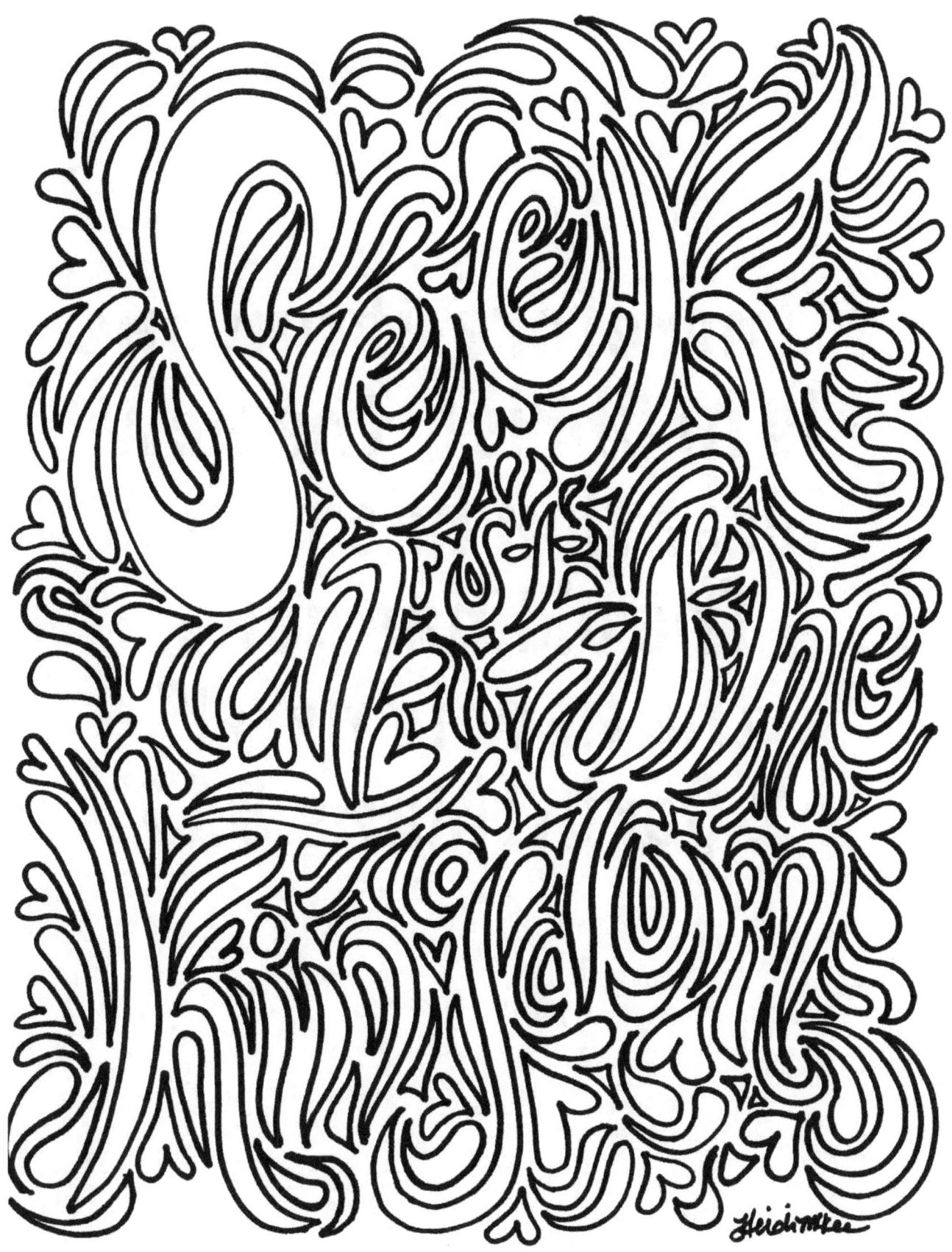

"Therefore, if anyone is in Christ, the new creation has come: The old has gone, the new is here!"
2 Corinthians 5:17

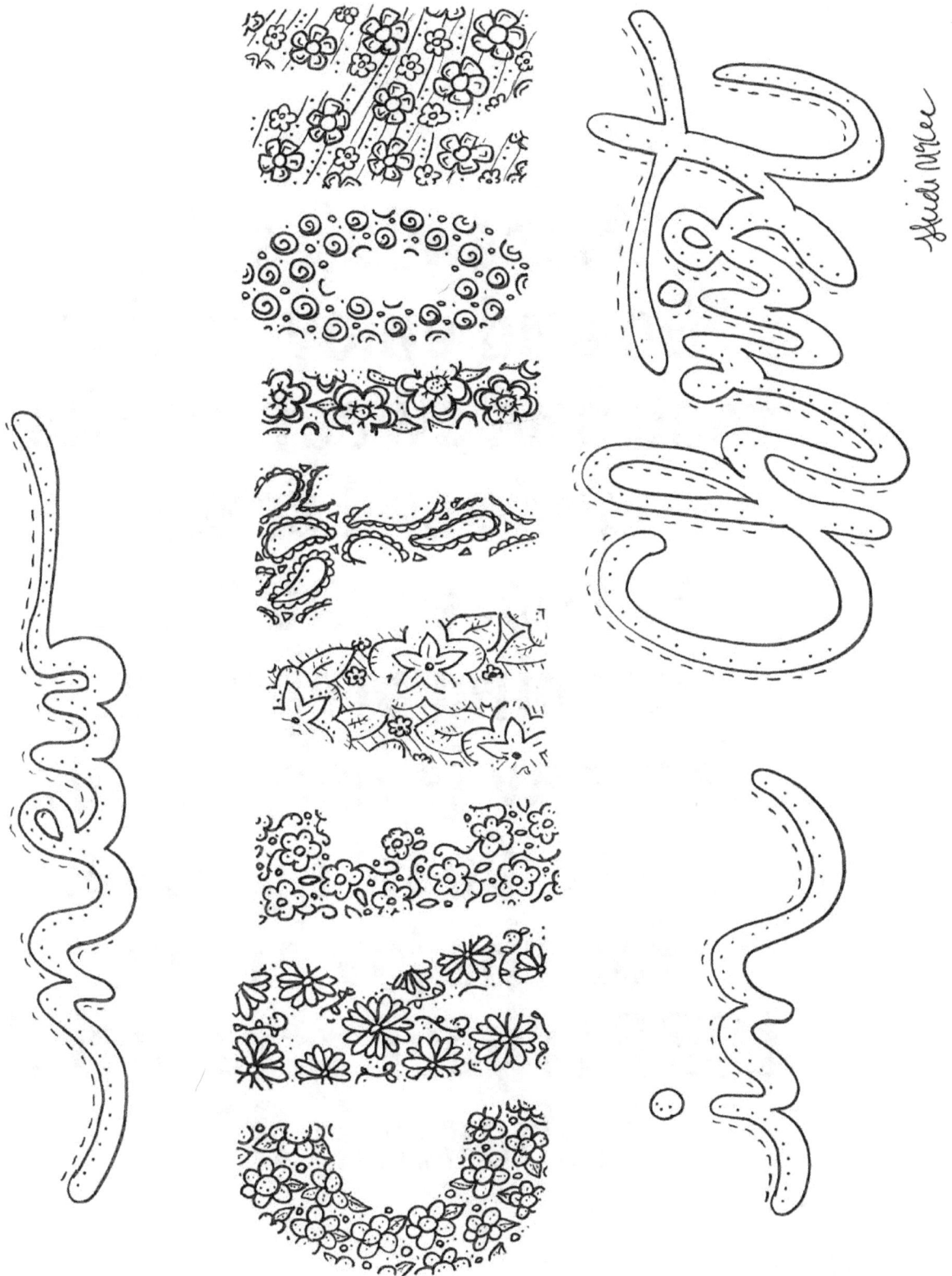

"Nehemiah said,
"Go and enjoy choice
food and sweet drinks,
and send some
to those who have
nothing prepared.
This day is holy to our
Lord. Do not grieve,
for the joy of the
LORD is your strength."
Nehemiah 8:10

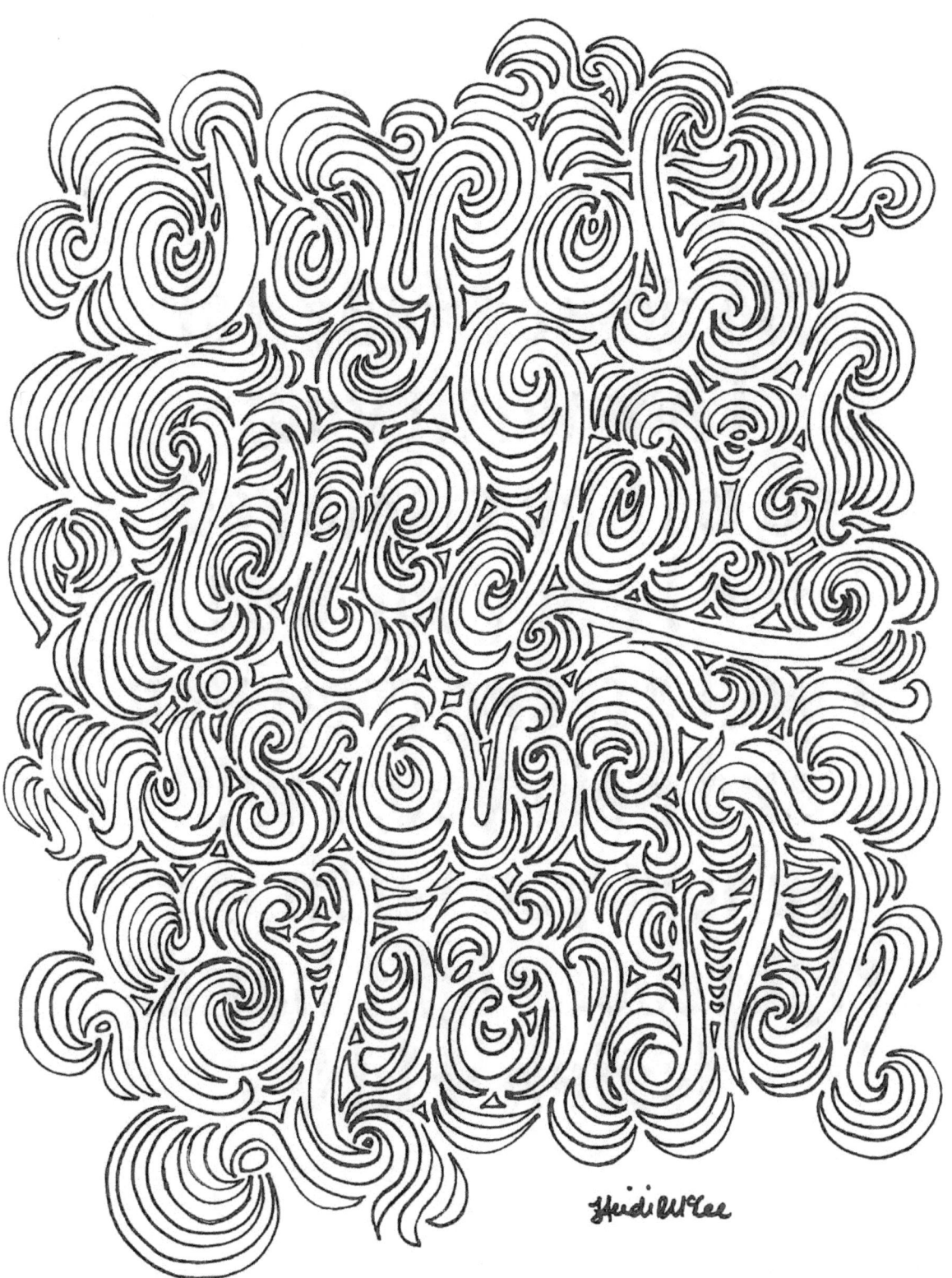

"So do not fear, for
I am with you;
do not be dismayed,
for I am your God.
I will strengthen you
and help you; I will
uphold you with my
righteous right hand."
Isaiah 41:10

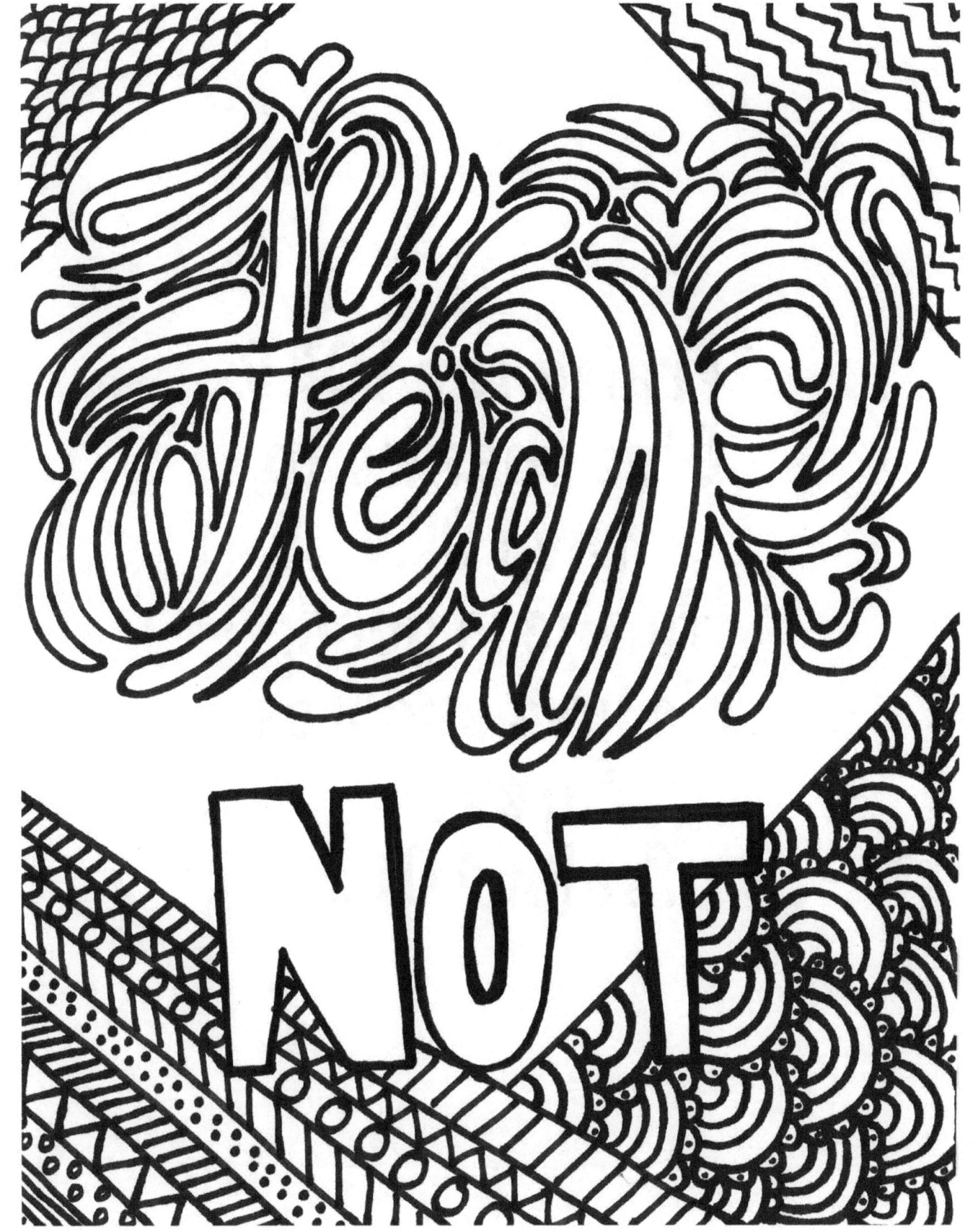

"Praise the LORD.
Give thanks to
the LORD,
for he is good;
his love endures
forever."
Psalm 106:1

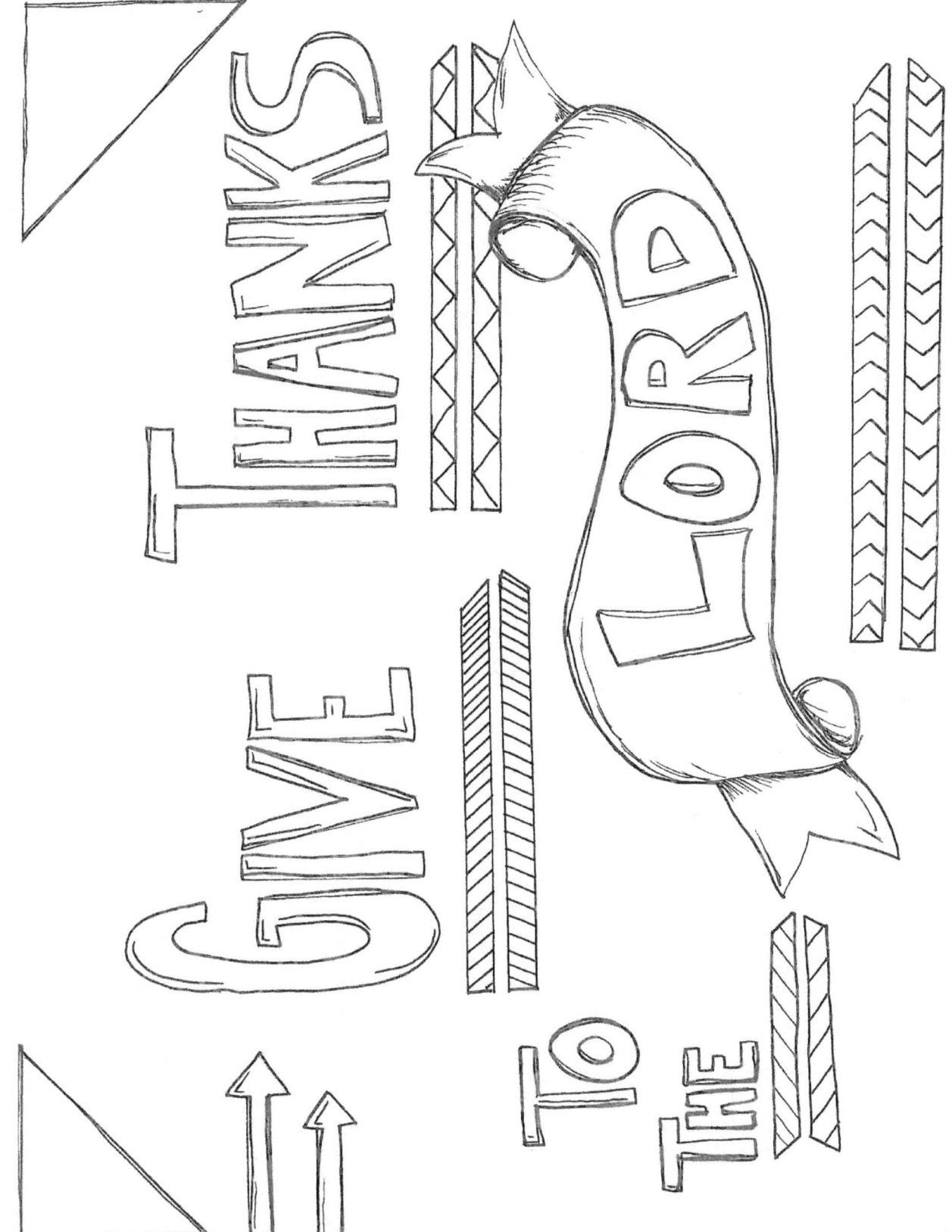

GIVE THANKS TO THE LORD